Emotional Intelligence

————— ✦✦✦✦ —————

The Complete Step-by-Step Guide on Self-Awareness, Controlling Your Emotions and Improving Your EQ

Table of Contents

Introduction:

A Step-by-Step Guide to Developing Emotional Intelligence

To define emotional intelligence (EI) as being aware of one's emotions and knowing how to control those emotions to build fruitful and empathetic relationships doesn't give you the full picture. The beauty in studying EI is to understand how to develop and use that emotional intelligence to improve your life. My goal in this book is to take you through the steps of how to do just that—to identify, develop and heighten your emotional intelligence to create stronger personal and professional relationships.

For clarity, let's take emotional intelligence beyond its definition and step into a greater understanding of what EI can do for you. Perhaps the best way to bring clarity to the term

Introduction: A Step-by-Step Guide to Developing Emotional Intelligence

"emotional intelligence" is first to dispel some of its mysteries and myths. Emotional intelligence is NOT a personality trait. People who have high EI aren't necessarily optimistic, agreeable, or always happy. EI goes deeper than your outward personality; it's almost like having an inherent ability to perceive emotions and respond in a way that benefits all parties. It's learning how to feel emotions, not just be able to identify or recognize them. Having high emotional intelligence is knowing how to harness emotional energy and turn it into predictable and positive outcomes.

In my book, *Emotional Intelligence: The Definitive Guide to Understanding Your Emotions, How to Improve Your EQ and Your Relationships,* I spent lots of time describing the term and the importance it played in your personal and professional relationships. So, for some of you, it might be a good idea to first read that book and my second book *Emotional Intelligence Mastery: How to Master Your*

Emotions, Improve Your EQ, and Massively Improve Your Relationships. They both offer a firm foundation on what is introduced in this book. Now that you've learned what Emotional Intelligence is and how it can influence your life, we're going to take you through a step-by-step guided tour of how to improve your emotional intelligence through a robust analysis of your emotions and that of those with whom you surround yourself.

In this step-by-step guide to emotional intelligence, you'll learn how to assess your EI, observe others emotions with a heightened awareness, practice control and focus on improving your EI, and create predictable outcomes that bring you greater success in life. Instead of ignoring or scoffing at the evidence of emotions, you'll learn how to follow the steps to change the course of your life and others by using those same emotions to make you more decisive and attractive.

Introduction: A Step-by-Step Guide to Developing Emotional Intelligence

Often, the best way to better understand a topic is to begin questioning your feelings on the matter. So, let's get personal, shall we? Let's make it all about you. Ask yourself the following:

1. What will develop a high emotional intelligence in you?

2. How will you know if you have a high emotional intelligence?

3. Why is it important to know what your emotional intelligence is, anyway?

4. When will you notice a difference in your life?

5. Where can you expect this greater emotional awareness to take you?

To know what developing a high emotional intelligence can do for you, it's helpful to know what it has done for others. Developing a high emotional intelligence has helped CEOs run huge corporations, national leaders gain public support, and creative artists reflect the values and truths of their times. As you work through the steps of this book, you'll begin to examine your personal EI and determine the things you'll need to do to climb to a higher standard of emotional communications. Some of you who already have high EI may not notice a significant difference, merely a little improvement here and there to lighten the load. However, those of you who have been ruled for decades by emotional outbursts or suffered social isolation because of poor EI, the changes you'll experience will be immediate.

As to where you can expect this greater emotional awareness to take you? Well, the possibilities are limited only by your ability to practice these steps daily to become an emotional intelligence mensa. Improving your EI can lead you to more stable relationships, greater professional achievements and a more intuitive understanding of how to respond to others and predict how they will react to you. In

short, increasing your emotional intelligence can
be life altering.

You don't have to be a road scholar to have high
emotional intelligence. In fact, there is no
correlation between having a high IQ and a high
EI. The size of your brain has little to do with
your ability to recognize and build your
emotional intelligence. It's more about the size
of your heart than the size of your brain. When
you approach others, how do you perceive them?
What feelings do you leave them with when they
leave your presence? It's more about feeling
with your heart than knowing with your mind.
That's what the following steps will show you—
how to control and apply your feelings and
emotions so that you will be perceived and will
see others in their absolute best light.

As you learn and follow the steps presented in
this book, you'll begin to see yourself and others
differently. Instead of jumping to conclusions
before knowing all the facts of the situation,

you'll find yourself stepping back and observing the other person's emotions. When, before, you would have made a rash decision based on irrational feelings, now you'll start to mull things over a bit more and imagine how your behavior might negatively impact others. That's called having emotional intelligence. So, join me on this tour, this step-by-step guide to helping you discover and develop your emotional intelligence.

Chapter 1:

Step #1—Assessing Your Emotional Intelligence

I f we can agree that Emotional Intelligence is important, how can you assess your EI? We have designed a little test for you that will give you an accurate idea of your Emotional Intelligence. Take a few moments to answer the follow questions, and then let's talk about your scores.

Emotional Intelligence Assessment

Answer the following questions and then tally up your score. At the end of the test, you'll know your Emotional Intelligence level.

1. You're riding in a taxi. You notice that the driver is taking many side streets, and you fear your charge will reflect his poor sense of direction. What do you do?

    a. Tap him on the shoulder and tell him you don't appreciate his attempt to rack up a higher tab.

    b. Let him know you are familiar with the area and ask him what he believes is the quickest route to take to get to your destination.

    c. Ignore him and decide never to use this company again.

    d. Refuse to pay the bill.

2. Your daughter has a friend in the neighborhood come over to play. When the friend leaves, your little girl begins to cry because she has no more money in her piggy bank. It appears the older child next door took advantage of your daughter and stole the money from her piggy bank. What would you do?

a. Listen to your daughter's story, and then share with her how something similar happened to you when you were little so she wouldn't feel so bad.

b. March right over to the neighbor's house with your daughter to tell the girl's mother and demand she gives back the money.

c. Let your little girl express her anger over her loss, and then together discover a way to prevent this from ever happening again.

d. Reprimand your daughter and refuse to give her any more allowance until she learns to take better care of her money.

3. You are trying to impress your boss and win the "salesperson of the year" award, but you're getting discouraged because

the last 20 calls you've made have been hang-ups. What do you do?

a. Try a different call tactic.

b. Quit

c. Stop trying to get so much attention for your performance.

d. Stop and consider what you are doing that could be hindering your opportunity to make the sale, and then try something you've learned that might be more efficient.

4. You're on your way to the movies with your significant other, and the driver in the car next to you cuts you off. Your significant other starts to fume—what do you do?

a. Encourage him to pull beside the other drive so you can yell obscenities.

b. Turn the radio up and sing to drown out your partner's swearing.

c. Tell him he gets way too mad when drivers cut him off, and then share with him how it happens to you all the time and you don't lose it.

d. Let him express himself, and then point out that the other driver could have been an out-of-towner or someone headed for the hospital.

5. You are trying to learn some new software on your computer, but the tutorial is not helping, and you're getting quite frustrated. What do you do?

a. You give it a rest for a while, and then ask a friend who is good with computers for help.

b. You vow never to use the computer again and shut it down.

      c. You decide to wait until you're in a better mood to try learning the new program.

      d. You choose to take a class on the software and be patient with yourself during the learning curve.

Scoring: Give yourself five points for every correct answer.

1.   Correct answer is b = 5 Points

2.   Correct answer is c = 5 Points

3.   Correct answer is d = 5 Points

4.   Correct answer is d = 5 Points

5.   Correct answer is d = 5 Points

If you scored 25 points, you have the highest Emotional Intelligence.

If you scored 20 points, you have more Emotional Intelligence than many.

If you scored 15 points, you need to work on your Emotional Intelligence.

If you scored 10 points or below, you have little awareness of your or others' emotions.

So, let's think about this brief assessment for a moment. How do you "feel" about the emotions this test stirred in you? What if I told you, no exact five-question test could demonstrate the level of your emotional intelligence? The five-question assessment has no validity, but now you're probably feeling a whole other set of emotions. You could be feeling frustration, confusion, tricked even. Any way you look at it, there are some emotions you have to deal with right now. So, now we can truly assess how you're thinking about these emotions.

Most people tend to over-rate their Emotional Intelligence level. Have you ever had bosses who considered themselves to be very tuned into their emotions and those of their employees, but who were actually living in an emotional wasteland?

Chapter 1: Step #1—Assessing Your Emotional Intelligence

All this thinking about emotions leads us to a different definition of Emotional Intelligence. Emotional Intelligence is how you think about and express your feelings. Taking it one step further, how do you use that information about your feelings to change your behavior and the behavior of others?

Taking a test isn't going to provide answers about feelings and emotions. Contemplating your feelings and how to control your emotions is what will give you an accurate gauge on your Emotional Intelligence. Not all emotions are black or white—many fill up that gray area of complex feelings that need more than a label to define them. For example, it's easy to identify a feeling of sorrow when your pet dies. However, can you distinguish the difference between frustration and anger? Do you know when you're feeling shame or is it embarrassment you're experiencing?

Complex emotions need reflection and thought to sort through and assess. That reflection is what eventually improves and strengthens your Emotional Intelligence. Learning to deal productively with your emotions helps you to identify and assess others emotions. Emotions are not to be confused with moods. Moods are, by nature, flighty and erratic. Emotions are truer, easier to think through and assess. Have you ever awakened in a bad mood, as if for no reason? You've had no conversation, no event yet in your day that could cause you emotional turmoil—you're just in a mood, right? It's helpful to understand as we go through these steps that we're not speaking of mood swings here, but rather discussing one's inner emotions.

Since Emotional Intelligence requires thought about your feelings, let's do that to develop a more accurate measurement of your EI. I'm going to give you some situations, and I want you to think about how you typically feel when you find yourself enmeshed in them. The first step in

Chapter 1: Step #1—Assessing Your Emotional Intelligence

assessing your feelings is simply recognizing or identifying them.

What did you feel when...

- Your best friend, once again, stood you up for a get-together?

- Your employer broke his/her promise to give you a pay increase?

- Your family member was very ill and in the hospital?

- You heard someone at your door at midnight, and you were all by yourself?

- Your significant other said they had a confession to make?

- Your mother or father expressed pride in your achievement?

- You wanted something so desperately but knew you could never have it?

- You lost your job or failed to get that promotion?

- Your sister or brother received rewards for something you knew you could do better?

- Your husband or wife forgot your birthday?

As you go through these issues, you will notice that some emotions are clearly defined, and others fall in that gray area. Emotions that you must think about are usually ones with layers of unresolved issues, ones that you have repeatedly stuffed down or ignored so as not to have to deal with them. By not pausing at the time to think through your emotions, you have stunted the forward progress of your Emotional Intelligence.

Assessing your Emotional Intelligence means asking yourself if you truly have a handle on your feelings. When you are emotional, do you react or stop to think things through? If your friend is hurting, do you avoid her company until she has worked through her problem, or do you stand by her and help her to resolve the emotional issue? All this is a part of your Emotional Intelligence. Every time you feel emotional, or you sense a high emotional state in others, think about what you are feeling and how best to manage those feelings to help yourself and others reach a positive outcome to the issue. It's the thinking that positively contributes to one's Emotional Intelligence. It's important to know how you process all the emotional information you absorb each day because it's in that processing that you can better asses your EI.

There are all sorts of tests that say they measure your Emotional Intelligence, but if your perception of self is somewhat skewed, isn't the information just more of the same? Most of us can't trust ourselves to be honest when it comes to evaluating our EI, so how valuable are any of these tests? If you're reading this book, you probably either sense that you need help with your emotions, or you have a desire to learn how to become more emotionally intelligent when it comes to making decisions. Either way, it doesn't matter. You've already taken the first step—you're thinking about the emotions you and others are feeling—you've worked through Step #1!

Chapter 2:

Step #2—Creating Emotional Awareness

Since our childhoods, most of us have been taught to categorize and judge our emotions and the emotions of others. What is omitted in our early training is how to be more aware of our emotions and how they affect our decisions, behaviors, and beliefs about ourselves and others. For example, you may have learned as a child that crying was bad. Consequently, as an adult, you rarely cry and especially not in public. If someone you trusted had taught you that crying was only a way your body allows you to let off some built-up steam and stress, then perhaps you would be more capable of handling your own tears and feel more comfortable around others when they feel the need to cry.

That's the first step in creating more emotional awareness. Let go of your past judgments and categories where you have conveniently tucked away the emotions with which you feel uncomfortable. When you have tears or see someone else tearing up, grab a tissue and experience the waterworks. You'll be surprised at how refreshed you will feel when you let yourself experience the honesty of your emotions without the need to try to explain or rectify the situation. Just feel the raw emotion. As you think about what you are feeling with the tears, most of them will probably just dry up on their own, and you'll be consumed with wonder about the feelings associated with the tears.

There's No Right or Wrong Time to Feel Emotions

The process of awareness is enhanced when you close the door on judgment and criticism. Keep in mind; there's not a right or wrong time to feel your emotions. The only thing that is wrong is deciding not to feel at all. When you allow yourself to feel and think about the emotions you are feeling; you have increased awareness of how to use your feelings to positively impact your life.

Emotional awareness also reveals patterns in behaviors and thoughts that help you to identify and link similar emotions to events that may be triggers for you. When you are aware of emotional patterns in yourself and others, you can teach yourself to use this emotional information in your relationships, decision-making, and know when you are reacting irrationally to a situation. Then, instead of experiencing the typical "knee jerk" actions that may have challenged you in the past, you'll know to pause and give yourself a bit more time to think things through. You'll use your emotions in a more logical manner.

Learn to Listen and Observe

While awareness is necessary, it's not the end-all to gaining more Emotional Intelligence. Okay, so you're aware that every time you sit down at your desk at work, you feel a knot in your stomach. So, what? If you have identified the feeling but haven't given yourself time to think about why you feel this way, then there's no hope of resolving the underlying issues.

Listening and observing your body's reaction to emotions enhances your awareness and increases the likelihood that you'll seek a remedy for the discomfort. What must you do to dissolve the knot in your stomach? Well, if your feelings are telling you that you don't like your job, then it may be time to choose another company or perhaps a different career path. If you break out in a sweat every time you give a presentation, maybe you need more practice to increase your confidence. Some emotions cannot be avoided or ignored, but when you are aware of their influence, you can take steps to manage them better. That's practicing higher Emotional Intelligence.

As you become more aware of your emotions, you'll want to ask yourself some questions during the "think through" process. Some of the questions that are helpful are as follows.

- How are these feelings contributing to my setbacks or successes?

- Am I unduly distracted by these feelings or emotions?

- How am I being challenged by these emotions to allow myself to move forward in a more positive manner?

- What will enhance my ability to manage these emotions and use them to create stronger personal and professional relationships?

- What positive responses and behaviors do I see from others who might be experiencing similar emotions?

Chapter 2: Step #2—Creating Emotional Awareness

As you learn to listen and observe yourself and others' outward display of their feelings, use the time to reflect on the emotions you are witnessing. Think about how you would have handled the emotional situation. Give yourself time to consider alternative behaviors. Suddenly your Emotional Intelligence has changed from being an "inside" thought process to an external action that causes you to behave differently in future situations. You've successfully linked your previous thoughts to future outcomes, making it easier to predict favorable results. Greater Emotional Intelligence is an amazing thing, don't you think?

Breaking the Habits of Low Emotional Intelligence

Having low Emotional Intelligence is habit forming. You've become accustomed to ignoring yours and others emotions and so it's easier to continue to do what you've always done—turn away and distract yourself with other things. If you give emotions any thought at all, it's usually to pass quick judgment and then busy yourself with another activity. This can be a habit that is challenging to break.

There are two common habits that those with low Emotional Intelligence frequently practice. They are either easily offended, or they easily offend. Either way, these two habits block your ability to become more emotionally aware and use your emotions to benefit yourself and others. Pay attention to your thoughts when you witness the emotions of others. Do you say to yourself, "Oh for heaven sake—suck it up?" If so, learn to reprogram your self-talk. Start by thinking to yourself, "I wonder what is causing them to feel this way? What can I do to help?" This is called empathy or putting yourself in another's shoes so that you can open new avenues of understanding. If you get your feelings hurt at the drop of a hat, take notice of your feelings. Ask yourself, "Did I do something wrong? What can I do next time to improve my response to this type of situation?"

Deriding yourself for your feelings doesn't work, and it does nothing to help you break either of these two habits that inhibit greater Emotional Intelligence. There is a message in every emotion, so you must search for the message. What are your feelings telling you? How will being more aware of these feelings in the future help you to change your behaviors and improve your relationships? Now you've established new habits, making it much easier to eliminate the old ones.

Learning to Hear Your Emotions

Once your awareness has increased, you'll notice that emotions can be quite apparent in your voice as well as your body. Many people who are feeling fearful or are experiencing a lack of confidence will get a shaky voice. Of course, anger will make your voice increase in volume and speed. Frustration, on the other hand, often raises your voice a few octaves. Sorrow or disillusionment usually lowers your pitch and volume. When someone is attempting to control their emotions, their voice can become slower, more stilted and pronounced.

Couple the voice with body language, and you'll soon be reading a whole novel of emotions in others as well as yourself. For example, if someone is holding their body rather stiffly and their rate of speech is slower with their words pronounced more distinctly, you can almost bet they are feeling some strong emotions—usually anger or frustration. When you have successfully read the emotions lurking just beneath the surface of your conversation, you can act accordingly to defuse the emotion. Take a deep breath, accept that there is something wrong, and then take the appropriate action. What a transformation. Now you've used your Emotional Intelligence to set a higher standard of behavior than you would have previously exhibited.

Getting Comfortable with Your Emotions

Did you ever think that you'd be using the words comfort and emotions in the same sentence? If you're not quite a believer yet, that you can become comfortable with your feelings and emotions, keep practicing. Like anything else, the more you allow yourself to think and experience your emotions, and the more empathy you have for others, the easier Emotional Intelligence becomes.

At first when you have increased your emotional awareness, expect a flood of emotions to come streaming through your previously damned-up wall. Not to worry! Take one emotion and feeling at a time and give yourself time to think about it—identify it—manage it. Then you'll be ready for the next one and the next one until you've managed to work through an entire parade of emotions. It also takes some energy, so be patient with yourself. Enhancing your Emotional Intelligence takes effort, and allowing yourself to fully feel your emotions for the first time can be a bit draining. Trust me; it'll get better.

Once you get comfortable with your emotions, it will be much easier to deal with the emotions of others. Empathetic understanding will be second nature to you, and you'll earn the respect and admiration of others who may have previously been out of reach. People are attracted to those with high Emotional Intelligence, even those who pride themselves on being quite logical minded. Everybody likes to be heard, understood, valued and appreciated. That's what Emotionally Intelligent people do, and that's why others seek to have what they recognize in Emotionally Intelligent people.

Very little else sets you apart more than your Emotional Intelligence. It is as powerful and persuasive as having an extremely high IQ. In fact, studies show that Emotional Intelligence is more likely to bring success and well-being than those with high IQs. The Center for Creative Leadership (CCL) studied why seemingly intelligent corporate leaders found their careers stalled when their abilities and skills should have dictated otherwise. After a study of more than 20,000 individuals in 2,000 organizations what they discovered was that there were three main reasons for this phenomenon—all related to Emotional Intelligence.

1. They had challenges handling change.

2. They found it difficult to work as a team.

3. They were incapable of developing strong working relationships.

Many CEOs have been relieved of their positions, not because of their lack of competence, but because of a lack of Emotional Intelligence. Furthermore, studies done by the Carnegie Institute of Technology showed that 85% of our success financially was due to how well we had learned to communicate, negotiate, and perform skills that required an awareness and understanding of others feelings and emotions. Just 15% of our financial success was due to our technical expertise and abilities.

Now that you're becoming more aware of the need to address your emotions and allow yourself to feel, let's look in the next chapter how you can move from chaos to control.

Chapter 3:

Step #3—Moving from Chaos to Control

People of high Emotional Intelligence experience just as much chaotic emotions as the next person, the difference is they have learned how to control the chaos of emotions that others let run amuck. They are aware of their emotions and feelings, but instead of burying them, they take a breath and examine their feelings to determine how best to manage the emotions in a positive and constructive way. Sure, they feel all the emotions with the exception that they don't react impulsively and let their emotions create chaos. They practice self-control.

The truth is, as humans we experience the emotions before we have time to think about why we feel as we do. Those with a high degree of Emotional Intelligence give themselves permission not to have all the answers, to search for another alternative to the problem that would be more positive and productive. Emotional Intelligence requires that we take a moment to analyze how the emotions we are feeling will influence the outcome of the situation and impact us and those around us. Emotionally Intelligent people are confident enough to give the issue some time to simmer—time for them to contemplate different perspectives.

Exercise C.O.N.T.R.O.L.

Let me share with you what I mean by C.O.N.T.R.O.L.

C = Consider the Consequences

What will be the result of your actions? If you react without thinking about the consequences, your choices may not provide you with the desired outcome.

O = Optimism

Practicing optimism allows you to get in front of the emotion with positive thinking, even a little humor if necessary. People with positive outlooks almost always get more positive results from the decisions they make.

N = Neutralize the Emotions

Thinking about emotions neutralizes their power and calms the feelings. Most extreme emotions carry quite a punch, so when you can take the power out of the punch, your emotional state calms down, and you can think more rationally.

T = Take Ten

Take ten seconds to pause and consider the what and why of your feelings. This brief little pause along with a few deep breaths will position you to think calmly and make all-around better choices.

Chapter 3: Step #3—Moving from Chaos to Control

R = Regulate

Regulate your reactions in emotional situations. Apply all the elements of control, and help yourself and others to move away from the chaos of emotionally charged situations.

O = Openly Accept

Openly accept that you are going to experience emotionally charged situations. It's how you respond in these circumstances that will enhance your Emotional Intelligence. Be open to doing things differently, to accepting your own and others' emotions, to a willingness to admit your mistakes and hold yourself accountable for the decisions you make.

L = Look for Alternatives

Look for alternative behaviors, actions, and solutions to problems rather than giving into the chaotic emotions that have ruled you in the past. When you reach a higher degree of Emotional

Intelligence, the alternatives will present themselves more clearly, and you'll be much more open to trying something different.

How Do You Get Control?

Good question! You get to control one moment at a time—one emotion at a time—one action at a time. As difficult as it might seem, there are some definite steps you can take to move from chaos to control.

1. Assume responsibility for your emotions and actions.

    - Here's that word "consequences" again, but you must learn to accept the consequences of your actions. Hold yourself accountable. Admit you've made mistakes so that you can correct those things next time.

    - Stop blaming others for your circumstances or dicey situations. Nobody should have the power to control your success but you. If you think they do, then you've given away too much of yourself—you've lost your inner strength and confidence.

- Put yourself in an emotional place that enables you to earn the respect of others. It's an incredible boost to know that others look up to you, that they depend on you to help them grow emotionally.

2. Know what's most important to you.

- What do you value? What do you believe? What are you absolutely not willing to compromise?

- Know what you believe to be morally right, and then refuse to cross that line.

- What is your ethics? Do the decisions you make reflect high morals and ethical behavior?

3. Reap all the benefits of calmness.

   - Pay attention to your emotions. Know what creates stress in your life, then decide how you plan to remove the stress. Take action to come to calm.

   - Stop the negative self-talk. If it takes writing down all your negative talk on a piece of paper to enable you to visualize the influence negative emotions have over your well-being, then write them down, rip them up, and dump them in the circular file.

   - Practice deep breathing. Get some physical exercise. Do whatever it takes to spend some of that emotional energy. Then enjoy the calm.

Chapter 3: Step #3—Moving from Chaos to Control

You'll know you've reached greater levels of Emotional Intelligence when the decisions you make are rarely rushed or filled with emotional baggage. When your self-talk is positive, and you stop judging and stereotyping others, that's a clear indication that your Emotional Intelligence is gaining ground. When people are drawn to you and share their situations with you in hopes of guidance, then you'll know you've made great strides in improving your Emotional Intelligence.

Some people are born more intuitive, and feeling than others and some learn to have greater Emotional Intelligence at an early age, but no matter how old you are and what your position in life is, you can strengthen your ability to control and manage your emotions. There is nothing that is so permanent that it cannot be changed even if it's just by a little here and there. Perhaps the situation cannot be changed, but you can modify the way you perceive it, the way you plan to handle it. On the other hand, if there is something that happens that you feel changes everything, there are ways to face that battle as well. Those with high Emotional Intelligence see possibilities when others see problems; they see opportunities when others see obstacles. The choice is yours. So, what's it going to be? Well, it depends on your Emotional Intelligence, which provides you with great motivation to improve your EI.

I've heard it said that the greatest predictor of future outcomes is past behaviors; however, I'm not so sure that's true. I believe the more accurate predictor of future outcomes is the level of your Emotional Intelligence. Are you willing to look at your emotions in the eye and say to yourself, what can I do differently today that will give me better results than I had yesterday? How can I use the emotions and feelings I am having to influence my life's outcomes and bring me greater success? The choices you make and the actions you take as a result of these questions are truly life altering. Improving your Emotional

Chapter 3: Step #3—Moving from Chaos to Control

Intelligence is what will be the best predictor of your future success.

Satisfaction in both your personal and professional life is more linked to Emotional Intelligence than almost anything else. More so than riches, IQ, or great careers, you'll find that Emotional Intelligence isn't too far behind the scenes of successful people. Our most memorable moments are teaming with individuals who have a high level of Emotional Intelligence. Think about when you felt the most loved, appreciated, valued, cherished, and needed, and then reflect on those who surrounded you in those moments. I'll bet you can identify many who had a high degree of Emotional Intelligence, right?

The Best Way to Control Yourself is to Help Others

Few things create more desire to perform at your peak, to reach heightened self-awareness, or to share the most love as others in your life who are willing to give the same back to you. Whether you have high Emotional Intelligence or yours is rather lacking at the moment, the people you find most attractive are usually those with high Emotional Intelligence. They somehow have the ability to draw people to them like wanderers to a warm fire on a cold winter's night.

We recognize Emotional Intelligence in others and want that for ourselves. You may not know what to call it, but you know there's something different about them that makes you enjoy their company. To examine your emotions and apply control over what might have been a turbulent past, observe and listen to those whom you recognize to have Emotional Intelligence. Watch how they monitor their emotions and express their feelings. Listen to how they encourage others to do the same. Do they take a little time to think things through before trying to resolve a problem? Do they value what others contribute in a meeting or a personal relationship? Then ask yourself how! How do they do what they do? Better yet, ask them to share their feelings with you. Emotionally Intelligent people don't mind opening up about their feelings. In fact, they usually welcome the opportunity.

Looking at the World through a Positive Lens

There was once two young men who were twins with entirely different outlooks on life. Although they had been raised by the same parents, in the same neighborhood, under the same economic situation, their futures reflected two completely different outlooks on the world. When asked why the one twin left home at such an early age and turned to using drugs, he responded, "Well, it was because of my parents and the neighborhood in which I lived." When asked why the other twin went on to college and became a successful businessman, he replied, "Well, it was because of my parents and the neighborhood in which I lived."

Each twin was raised in the same environment under the same circumstances, but with obviously different degrees of Emotional Intelligence. Each chose how they felt about their life's circumstances and how those feelings would influence the decisions they made in their lives. They even experienced the same emotions. What was different was how they chose to think about and control those emotions that set each twin's life path.

So, let me ask you—what will you choose? Will you choose chaos or control? Then ask yourself, what influence will these choices have over the rest of your life?

Chapter 4:

Step #4—Redirecting Your Focus

W hat you choose to focus on is one of the most critical elements to being able to manage your emotions effectively. Whatever emotion you are focusing on at the time, you are actually feeding it, making it more powerful, and giving it enduring strength. By focusing on the negative feelings in your life, you not only strengthen them, but you weaken the positives. What you feed becomes stronger; what you starve gets weaker. Your emotions are rarely stagnating; they are either growing stronger or becoming weaker. The main part of the word "emotion" is "motion."

Your body feels the emotion before your mind comprehends its intensity or purpose. To prove my point, try a little experiment. Turn the corners of your mouth in a smile and begin to chuckle. Now strengthen that chuckle into full-blown laughter. It won't take long before your mind begins remembering something that gave you a giggle, and in just a matter of minutes, the positive is set into motion. Admit it; you weren't necessarily thinking about a happy moment before you began to laugh, right? As you focused on the real laughter, your thoughts followed with a happy memory.

The same can be said for clapping your hands and singing a happy tune. There's something about clapping your hands that won't allow you to feel depressed. Focus on the motion of clapping and the happy words to the song, and soon your outlook will be happy. It's like putting the positive in motion. Whatever feeling you focus on and feed becomes stronger. You don't necessarily have to be right in the middle of a positive experience to feel positive emotions; you just need to engage your mind and decide to be happy and remember something that makes you smile.

Have you ever had a shared story or joke with a family member or best friend and every time you begin to talk about it around others you just can't control your laughter? Because many in the group didn't experience the same event you did, they might not get the humor in the story, but it doesn't really matter because you and your friend are both so into the memory you turn into dribbling idiots and end up needing a tissue to wipe away the tears of laughter.

I shared one of these memories with my mother about a time my father wanted to go swimming but didn't have a suit. So, Mom and I went to the store and purchased a one-size-fits-all canary yellow swimsuit for him. What we discovered was that the clerk wasn't exactly truthful about the one-size-fits-all thing. After 30 minutes of desperate pulling and stretching, with a myriad of loud grunts and groans, my father exited the bathroom with a suit that showed every vulgar bump and wrinkles imaginable. With each step, the suit began to roll and creep down until he then resembled the Norge refrigerator repairman with his exposure getting more critically dangerous by the moment.

Oh, and I forgot to mention that my x mother-in-law was also witness to this bizarre event, and the expression on her face was that of shock and awe. To this day, I cannot share this story, especially in the presence of my mother, without doubling over with laughter. In fact, even seeing a one-size-fits-all sign in a clothing store is enough to set us off.

My point in telling this story is that you can decide to experience whatever emotion you focus on at the time. When I want to alleviate stress or depression, I often dredge up the memory of dad's most unflattering swim attire. If I really want to cement the feeling, I pick up the phone and call Mom, and we sputter on the phone for half an hour about the incident. If you want to magnify your focus on a feeling, share it in a story with others.

In Tony Robbins' book "Awaken the Giant Within," he presents the idea that the only reason people are motivated to do anything is to change the way they feel. They want to feel powerful, so they purchase a luxury car or a big house. They want to feel beautiful, so they lose weight or buy an expensive suit or dress. What many people fail to realize is that you can feel those emotions right now. Just decide to feel. You are already powerful and beautiful; you don't have to wait for something to happen to create those feelings. It's an amazing thing, but you can feel all those things with nothing changing in your life except your perspective.

If you want to feel like a giving person, give. If you want to be perceived as powerful, act powerfully. Not long ago, there was a young man who conducted an experiment. He hired a bunch of people to follow him through the streets of New York City with camera crews and act like an enthusiastic entourage. Thinking he must be a celebrity, complete strangers approached him on the street and began asking for his autograph. Viola, he was a star because he acted like a star.

Another example of creating emotions was when a man stood before marathon runners wearing a t-shirt that said "Free Hugs." People were approaching the end of the marathon and were worn out from the experience. They visibly wore the look of exhaustion on their faces and bodies. As they crossed the line almost ready to collapse, the young gentleman approached them with his arms held out and a huge smile on his face, ready to celebrate their efforts with a free hug. Their physical transformation was stunning. After they had got over the initial confusion, they shared the young man's big smile, held out their arms to welcome the hug, and shared a warm embrace that was both fun and energizing. Suddenly, their focus was on the hug of celebration instead of their aching bodies. Their focus was on the accomplishment instead of sore muscles and tired feet.

Let your body lead the way to open your mind's focus on all the possibilities of achieving greater Emotional Intelligence. Redirect your focus and let it lead the way to create Emotional Intelligence. Instead of burying your feelings, celebrate them, use them to push you to maximum performance, more meaningful relationships, and greater satisfaction in life. If it's up to you to forge your own path, why not make it a positive experience by focusing on all that is right and good. It doesn't mean that you will never feel the negatives, but they won't be strong enough to take control of your destiny.

Make Slaves of Your Negative Emotions

Just like you can use your positive feelings and emotions, you can also learn to use the negative emotions when they arise. For example, if you are aware of your negative emotions and recognize their patterns, then use them to improve yourself. Like that knot in your stomach, we discussed earlier that happened whenever you sat down at your desk at work, use it to motivate you to get another job or change your career to one that is more pleasing.

It takes courage to make slaves of your negative emotions. Why? Because negatives can be strong motivators for change, and change rarely happens without some struggle. Once you have a clear grasp on your feelings and understand how they can influence your life, you'll be willing to go through a time of discomfort to get to a better place. Suddenly, the tables will turn. Instead of being a slave to your negative emotions, you make them slaves to your actions and behaviors. Use them to push you to excellence.

First, you need to focus on the emotion, then on how you need to change your perspective, and lastly on your desired outcome. If you let the negative emotions control you, your focus will be limited and stifled. Remember, what you focus on becomes stronger, and everything you focus on is your choice. It's quite a freeing notion, this whole focus idea, wouldn't you say? If you want to wallow in self-pity, it's your choice. If you want to enjoy the positive feelings of a higher level of Emotional Intelligence, that's your choice as well.

Improving Your Ability to Focus

Remember the story of that marathon runner? When you are exhausted, your inability to focus will be evident in the choices and decisions you make. To improve your focus, get lots of sleep. It's difficult to feel positive when you're getting only a few hours of interrupted sleep each night. Your mind becomes foggy, and you begin to question every decision.

Next, eat properly. If your body is the first to indicate your feelings, then make sure it's strong. Eat healthy food that feeds the mind and muscles. Avoid overeating and creating a sluggish system that can barely focus on getting out of bed in the morning. There are certain foods that fuel thought—eat more of those. I can tell you; they usually don't come prepackaged or in the form of frozen dinners or salty snacks.

Get plenty of exercise to burn off the unwanted negative emotions and encourage you to focus on a healthier lifestyle. It's much easier to feel positive emotions when you know you're looking your best. Exercise and healthy food create "feel good" reactions in the mind and body. Being physically fit released chemicals and endorphins that expand your thinking and encourage better focus and greater cognitive thought.

Whatever you do, do it now. Don't wait until you look better, feel better, have achieved more success in your job, or have found that one-in-a-million relationship. Remember, it's a decision, so decide now to focus on feeling positive and rejuvenated. Focus on where you want to be instead of where you are. Focus on what will happen when you achieve Emotional Intelligence.

Chapter 5:

Step #5—Practicing a Daily Dose of Emotional Intelligence

We're such an instant society, always so busy running here and there that we rarely take the time to simply sit and reflect upon our feelings. In fact, just reading it might make some feel like they've returned to the '70s era where people walked the streets passing out flowers and sitting on the curb chanting. Who knows, perhaps that was the beginning of us thinking about Emotional Intelligence, and we lost touch with our feelings somewhere along the way.

As much as I believe Emotional Intelligence plays a significant role in all our lives, I too let my busy life get in the way of taking a few moments out of each day to focus on my feelings. Most people's lives are consumed by family, friends, careers, financial worries, and just everyday stuff that gets in the way of taking a little time for ourselves. At the end of a busy day, all we can think about is unplugging and turning into mindless little television zombies. The only emotions we want to reflect on at the end of the day is how we're going to address our exhaustion.

Well, here's a thought. What if that exhaustion is caused by your inability to take time for yourself? What if your day flowed much smoother and your energies were revived because you gave yourself a daily dose of Emotional Intelligence? You'd be amazed at how a few minutes escape each morning and afternoon would make such a difference in your energy level. Unresolved or misunderstood emotions can take their toll on your energy level.

There are three ways to deal with your feelings. Some people are clueless when it comes to understanding their emotions. They don't deal with their feelings because they refuse to consider the fact that they even have any emotions. Instead, they plow through life telling themselves they're loners, that they feel entirely comfortable being alone. Then, there are those people who are aware they have emotions and feelings that sometimes may be getting in the way of their relationships, but they don't know what to do with them. Instead of discovering how to deal with their emotions, they push them aside and make weak promises that things will get better when they are more financially stable, or when they lose weight or when they get a better job or a nicer car. What they don't realize is that their low Emotional Intelligence is what could be keeping them from greater achievement. If you've been putting off dealing with your emotions until tomorrow, consider this, tomorrow never comes. You're always in today—today is the time to practice Emotional Intelligence.

Then there are the ones, maybe just like you, who are seeking to improve your Emotional Intelligence by learning how to practice empathy, understanding, and awareness of yours and others' emotions. Stop reacting every time you have an emotional crisis, and start responding by giving your emotions some further thought. That's the difference between reacting and responding. When you respond to an emotional situation, you have already given it some thought. You have compared the feelings you are now having to others you have had in the past. You had already asked yourself when you experienced similar feelings how you planned to handle them in the future. Now, the future is here, and you are better prepared for the successful management of your emotions. You have just increased your Emotional Intelligence.

Practice Makes More Perfect Practice

It's important to understand that increasing your Emotional Intelligence is a lifelong endeavor.

It's not something you "get" today, wipe your brow and let out a sigh of relief that you have finally reached your peak. Emotional Intelligence is a mountain or understanding and awareness that has no peak. You will never reach the top; however, each day brings you new vistas of serenity and calm experiences that clear your vision and prepare you for your next climb.

This is a tough one for those who pride themselves on perfection because you will never reach the perfect level of Emotional Intelligence. What is possible is that each day you think about your feelings and allow yourself to contemplate how you will do things differently next time, then place yourself in social and professional environments that enable you to practice dealing with yours and others emotions; you gain ground. If it helps you, think of Emotional Intelligence as being a mountain with many lookout points, and you get to see a whole new, panoramic view every day.

Chapter 5: Step #5—Practicing a Daily Dose of Emotional Intelligence

Talking about practicing Emotional Intelligence isn't enough; now it's time for some sound practice. First, practice on yourself. Once you've given some thought to your feelings, to why you reacted a certain way in an emotionally charged situation, then step out and practice your Emotional Intelligence on others. Observe the facial expressions and body language of a group you are in, and when someone seems stressed question them further about what is causing their hurt or pain. It could be they are on an emotional high, and that's a good time to ask them to share their experience as well. Celebrate their happy event with them. Enjoy their success or experience, their joy, and laughter. Emotions aren't always bad, you know. Some are over-the-top fantastic, and you can now share those feelings while you practice your Emotional Intelligence.

Creating a Safe Environment

If practicing your Emotional Intelligence is going to be a complete turn-around for you, make sure you create a safe environment. Begin practicing with people you trust. You may even share with them how you are feeling, that's a wonderful way to practice. Choose individuals who care about you and want to see you succeed. A word of warning, these may not be your bar buddies or your co-workers. If you are going to explore your feelings and share your goals with another, make sure it is someone with high Emotional Intelligence. They will be the ones who will show you empathy and understanding, and you will be able to learn from them how to handle your emotions.

It can be difficult to trust your emotions when you've never even admitted you have any, or when you've prided yourself on not showing them. So, when you first come out, so to speak, do so with people who are not emotionally starved or isolated from their feelings. Once you have thought about your feelings, you'll need to trust them so that you can be encouraged to step outside your routine and show empathy to yourself and others.

You're on the precipice of change, and change requires things of you that might be difficult and challenging. Keep at it; the payoff is incredible. Once you experience successful strides in building your Emotional Intelligence, you'll never want to go back to that person you were yesterday who felt something was missing. There will be a void that finally begins to close, and a completeness within yourself that you've never had before.

That's one advantage of transformation; you can look back and see how far you've come; enjoy the journey. Others who have always had a high degree of Emotional Intelligence might never appreciate what they have quite as much as those who have to work hard to get it. What takes more work to accomplish is usually appreciated more than what comes naturally or easily. You've worked hard and earned your success, and that's a plus in my book.

Expect the Unexpected

What will begin to happen will be just short of miraculous. If you have been a loner in the past, and you start to gain ground with your Emotional Intelligence, you'll soon find yourself attracting friends, and people that you previously felt were out of your league. If you felt trapped in a "go nowhere" job, you'll be more willing to take a risk and step out to search for something that is more suitable to your newly gained Emotional Intelligence. In fact, you may have people come to you wanting you to join their team. The more Emotional Intelligence you get, the more you understand and empathize with yourself and others, the more you'll change into that person you always wanted to become.

Chapter 5: Step #5—Practicing a Daily Dose of Emotional Intelligence

Reaching greater heights of Emotional Intelligence is directly proportionate to how much you practice empathizing and understanding yours and others feelings. Practice a little and gain a little ground each day. Practice a lot, and you grow by leaps and bounds. It's all about choice, and the choice is yours. You set your limits and boundaries.

When you build your Emotional Intelligence, you will experience the most unexpected occurrences. People will begin asking for your opinion, and "surprise—surprise," you'll look forward to sharing your ideas and feelings. You may become the "go to" guy in office meetings. You might get brave and introduce yourself to an attractive stranger at a party, and he or she welcomes the intrusion with open arms and enticing conversation. You might be able to save the rocky relationship you are currently in, returning to your first feelings of love and admiration. Emotional Intelligence brings more surprises than you can imagine, so take a deep breath and get ready for the ride of your life.

Chapter 6:

Step #6—Predicting & Preventing Outcomes

In every aspect of our lives, it has been studied and proven that those with higher Emotional Intelligence can predict more positive outcomes in their personal and professional endeavors. Let's examine the influence of Emotional Intelligence from early adolescence to adulthood.

Predicting Academic Success

When children move into puberty, their hormones spur on the whole gamut of emotional experiences. To say that these emotions and feelings can be somewhat distracting is an understatement. If you begin to develop Emotional Intelligence at an early age, you are better prepared to manage these emotions and focus on academics successfully. Students who have a high Emotional Intelligence are calmer,

more satisfied with their social networks, feel
more supported by their family and friends, and
can successfully handle the anxiety that comes
with test taking and peer pressure.

Because early positive perceptions and beliefs
about yourself are the most important elements
in the development into stable adulthood, those
who learn Emotional Intelligence in their youth
are more likely to continue to gain more EI as
they mature. Emotional Intelligence positions
them for future management and leadership
roles as they enter the workplace.

Influence of EI on Your Health and Well-being

Doctors Schutte and Malouff, researchers in the
area of Emotional Intelligence conducted a study
in 2007, where they researched the correlation
between Emotional Intelligence and physical
health. What they found was that people with
high   Emotional   Intelligence   made   better

decisions and were less likely to use alcohol, drugs, and food as a way to self-medicate and handle unresolved emotional issues. Continual unresolved emotional issues cause a great deal of physical and mental stress, which can take its toll on your overall health. Learn how to address your feelings and emotions, and your physical health gets a giant boost. The less stress you feel, the more you can focus on the positive goals you want to achieve.

Developing More Complex Relationships

What has been developed, whether low or high Emotional Intelligence, in school, will be a good indication of what to expect as you begin to seek more complex personal and professional relationships. Those with higher Emotional Intelligence are more likely to build secure, stable, and more satisfying interpersonal relationships, says a study by Yale professors Mayer and Salovey, in 1999 study.

Chapter 6: Step #6—Predicting & Preventing Outcomes

It stands to reason, that when you have a high Emotional Intelligence, you are more able to avoid arguments and fights with your significant other. Your outlook on life is more positive, and you are in touch with yours and your partner's feelings. Most people with high Emotional Intelligence are less aggressive and have a calm, peaceful manner, which is much more conducive to a long-term, rewarding relationship.

Emotional Intelligence in the Workplace

Emotionally Intelligent people tend to make better choices when they decide on a career path, so they avoid much of the job-hopping and career changes that plague others whose decisions are impaired by emotions and feelings of which they are unaware. The benefit to making positive initial choices is that they experience greater job satisfaction and have more years to climb that ladder of success and to grow into a leadership role that brings with it more power and financial gain.

People enjoy being close to those with high Emotional Intelligence; therefore, they receive greater peer support and higher supervisor reviews. This also brings with it more pay increases and higher commissions. Salespeople with high Emotional Intelligence usually experience less rejection and more sales because they sell with empathy and understanding. It's a proven fact that people buy from those they like, and people like those with high Emotional Intelligence. There is also less burnout experienced by people with high Emotional Intelligence. Their energy levels are higher and they are more positive about their position in life, so there is less complaining and exhaustion at the end of their workday.

Emotionally Intelligent Leaders

Professors Freshman and Rubino, who was also Director of the Health Administration Program at California State University, held a study in 2002, showing that high Emotional Intelligence is a critical component of those in management and leadership roles. They discovered that people with high Emotional Intelligence experienced less turnover in the workplace and benefited from more productivity. When workers are not distracted or discouraged by overbearing and unsupportive leaders, they are much more positive and productive.

Here are a few examples of companies that have significantly benefited by incorporating Emotional Intelligence into their corporate structure.

- Sheraton—when Sheraton decided to include an Emotional Intelligence program, guess what happened? Their market share climbed by a whopping 24 percent.

- Pepsi—as Pepsi began to study the results of executives with high Emotional Intelligence, what they found was that their productivity was 10% greater than those with low Emotional Intelligence. They also discovered that they benefited from 87% less turnover. To put these figures into dollar amounts, what this meant to the Pepsi Corporation was an incredible 3.75 million in value and a 1,000% increase in their return on investment.

- Loreal—Loreal was another company who stepped out to examine what all the fuss was about regarding this Emotional Intelligence thing. What they found when investigating their salespeople was that those with high Emotional Intelligence sold 2.5 million more than those with lower EI.

When managers and leaders focus on good communications and pay attention to and support the feelings of their people, these reported financial gains make perfect sense. Executives who not only pay attention to what is said but also to what is not said, are far ahead of the game. When they can clearly see the stress on the faces of their employees and read the body language of workers who may be suffering from overwork or a lack of recognition, they can remedy these situations before the emotions can negatively impact production.

Managers and leaders who proactively engage their employees instead of reactively trying to put out the fires can spend more time in visionary pursuits that maintain their executives and company position as the industry's top dogs. It's no accident that Pepsi and Loreal have been leaders in their respective industries for over a hundred years. It's by design; it's by incorporating the ideas of those with high Emotional Intelligence that have given them marketplace longevity.

Taking Preventative Measures

As much as high Emotional Intelligence can predict positive outcomes to people's future, it should also be the encouraging element for you to take preventative measures to ensure you experience greater success. If you have suffered setbacks in your relationships or career, isn't it great to know that you can now take preventative measures to put you on a more successful path? Taking just a few minutes from your day to practice thinking about your feelings and how you can apply Emotional Intelligence in your decision making is being proactive in taking preventative measures that can help you to have more positive outcomes.

If you want to be more productive, then deal with the emotions before they deal with you. Do a little preventative maintenance and be one minded. When it's time to think about your feelings, do that. Then, when it's time to work you can do that without being distracted by anger or frustration that interferes with your job.

Chapter 6: Step #6—Predicting & Preventing Outcomes

Ten Way to Prevent Negative Outcomes

1. Speak your mind. Be honest with yourself about your emotions and feelings. Don't interrupt your self-talk with negative comments. Refuse to trivialize your feelings; they are real and they can be used to create more positive outcomes.

2. Live in the present. Stop worrying about yesterday, and give your feelings and emotions your full attention right now. The only time you should think about the past in when making decisions on how to better handle your current feelings. If you practice Emotional Intelligence and you have poor results, give yourself time to improve. Don't quit!

3. Find connections between past emotions and current feelings. How you feel about today is probably a result of what

happened to you in the past. Allow yourself to make the connection so that you can prevent more adverse outcomes.

4. Take thought breaks. Make a habit of taking breaks to think—just like some people take a coffee break. It will relax and rejuvenate your mind. You've heard that some executives take power naps. Why not take a thinking nap? Let your mind focus on your feelings and then find a solution to a pressing problem. Decide how to use your feelings to create more positive outcomes in your life.

5. Let your body speak. Listen to what your body is trying to tell you. If you are getting frequent headaches and stomach aches, it might mean that it's time for you to use your Emotional Intelligence and deal with your feelings in a way that will relieve your body of having to do all the work.

6. Clear your self-perceptions. If you aren't
    sure you are getting an accurate reading
    on yourself, ask a trusted friend to help
    you out with your self-analysis. Take an
    inventory of your perceptions. Ask a
    close friend how they perceive you. You
    might be surprised when you hear what is
    said.

7. Emotions are powerful. Sometimes, if
    emotions are not properly dealt with,
    they express themselves in other ways.
    One of the ways is in our dreams. You
    may want to try recording your dreams.
    What are your dreams trying to tell you?
    Do you have a recurring dream that
    might have some significant meaning?

8. Daily inventory. Take a daily inventory of
    your feelings. This is a good way to begin
    thinking about your emotions and
    gaining Emotional Intelligent. Ask
    yourself how you are feeling today? What

is different about today than yesterday? What will be different about tomorrow than today? Doing this allows you to plan how you can create more positive future outcomes.

9. Create a thought journal. If you are having trouble focusing on your feelings, write down your feelings in a reflection journal. There's something about writing that makes your mind slow down and focus.

10. Don't dwell on the negatives. Concentrate on the feelings, not the adverse event or outcome. If the feelings are negative, deal with the feelings—not the event or result of those feelings.

If all this is a bit too touchy-feely for you, if you think that thinking about feelings sounds weak, then consider this. Scientists, professors, national speakers and authors, even presidents have used Emotional Intelligence to achieve greatness. There was nothing soft about their positions or methods of leadership. Those same leaders with high Emotional Intelligence have helped us treat severe mental illness, taught us physics and calculus, led their industries in production, written books that helped thousands of people reach peak performance, and led us through wars. You'll be in good company when you chose to use higher Emotional Intelligence.

Conclusion

Thank you for downloading *Emotional Intelligence: The Complete Step-by-Step Guide on Self-Awareness—Controlling Your Emotions and Improving Your EQ.* We've given you a lot to think about—most importantly, how you can use your Emotional Intelligence to achieve greater successes in your life. Practicing these six steps to success will help you build positive personal and professional relationships, make better decisions, and find greater satisfaction in your career choices. A new and exciting world of opportunity is about to open up to you as you gain Emotional Intelligence.

I hope we have helped to change your perceptions and to think about how to manage your emotions and feelings. Emotions can cripple you or empower you; the choice is yours. The steps you have learned in this book will help you as you journey through some of your unresolved feelings and emotions. If the reading of this book leaves you hungry for more information, you might want to read some of my other works. Check out *Emotional Intelligence: The Definitive Guide to Understanding Your Emotions, How to Improve Your EQ and Your Relationships*, and *Emotional Intelligence Mastery: How to Master Your Emotions, Improve Your EQ, and Massively Improve Your Relationships*.

Obviously, there is a recurring theme in these works, and that is my belief that emotions and feelings matter. Feelings are core to our most basic needs. Feelings drive us, motivate us, and inspire us to achieve. Emotions created by those feelings also have tremendous influence in our life's outcome. Emotions in themselves are not good or bad; it's how we deal with them that determines whether they have a positive or negative impact. The important thing for you to remember is that you are in the driver's seat. The feelings belong to you. Either you chose to control your emotions, or you chose to let them control you. What's it going to be?

We are all born with different degrees of Emotional Intelligence, just as we are born with different levels of IQ. Even though our Emotional Intelligence is inherent, it doesn't mean it cannot be increased and improved. That's what this book was all about, adopting ways to create high Emotional Intelligence. You are now victim to your knowledge. After reading this book, it will be most difficult for you to return to an emotionally devoid life. Having journeyed with me through the pages of this book, the most logical progression will be to put these six steps into action and follow these proven strategies to lead you to a greater empathy and understanding of yours and others emotions and feelings.

As you focus on your future of higher Emotional Intelligence, I look forward to hearing from you about all the positive outcomes you'll be experiencing. It will also be interesting to hear

Chapter 6: Step #6—Predicting & Preventing Outcomes

you share your feelings and emotions about all the unexpected things that will happen to you along the way. The growth won't be immediate and you'll have your share of challenges, but your increased Emotional Intelligence will help you to weather the storms that working through some of these emotions may create.

Don't wait to work on the steps presented in this book; do it today. As soon as you finish reading, set this book down and take a moment or two to reflect on your feelings. Ask yourself how you are feeling after having finished the book. Where do you expect this information to take you? What do you think will change when you begin to practice more Emotional Intelligence in your personal and professional life?

Don't be surprised when your friends and family members notice a real difference in your manner and outlook. Basque in the added attention you will receive when you put these steps to work for you and begin to make choices and decision based on sound emotions and feelings.

I hope you're ready to enjoy all the benefits of increasing your Emotional Intelligence, of becoming more aware of yours and others feelings, and reaping the rewards in store for you as you move through life with more empathy and understanding. Who knows, sharing your feelings might become so second nature to you that you'll want to share how you felt as you read these books and encourage others to read them as well.

Thank you for taking the time to read this book. If you believe it helped you to get in touch with your feelings and emotions, to gain more knowledge about how to improve your Emotional Intelligence, please take just a few more moments to post a review. It would be so appreciated, and you'd be in a position to help others raise their Emotional Intelligence as well.

Chapter 6: Step #6—Predicting & Preventing Outcomes

Thank you once again, and congratulations on all the improved relationships, better decisions, and greater opportunities I know you will experience after having practiced these six steps to improve your Emotional Intelligence.

Printed in the USA
CPSIA information can be obtained
at www.ICGtesting.com
LVHW010238150823
755266LV00006B/170